A souvenir guide

Croft Castle and Parkland

Herefordshire

C000263205

National Trust

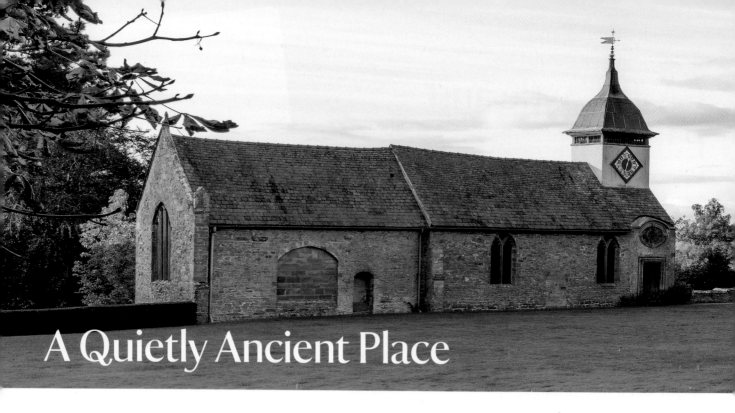

A Quietly Ancient Place

Croft Castle is unique among the castles and fortified homes of Herefordshire for having survived and been lived in by members of a single family, the Crofts, since the Norman Conquest, apart from an interval of 177 years.

The castle is approached through the tranquil, deeply rural landscape of Herefordshire. The current estate of 644 hectares (1,591 acres) is much reduced from its original size. The castle is one of only three of Herefordshire's 111 castles and moated sites to be lived in after the Civil War. Croft Castle and the county's other defences recall centuries of conflict along the Welsh Marches. High above the castle is the Iron Age hill fort of Croft Ambrey from where the Roman Camp hill fort on the Malvern Hills can just be seen. Croft Castle is a place where 21st-century visitors can immerse themselves in the turbulent history of this special area.

The earliest castle in the field to the west of today's structure began as a simple motte-and-bailey castle, later rebuilt as a stone-walled manorial complex; this was described in 1535 by John Leland as 'somewhat rokky, dyched and waullyd castle-like'.

Its late 1580s transformation was carried out by Sir James Croft who adapted the castle to become a more elaborate, brick-built Elizabethan house, probably surrounded by formal terraced gardens. The house lasted almost a century until its near destruction during the Civil War. Following the Restoration of Charles II, Herbert Croft inherited a building in desperate need of repair, but partly for his loyalty to the crown during the Civil War, he was financially rewarded by being elevated from Dean of Hereford Cathedral to its Bishop by the king.

After bankruptcy, the Croft family were forced to sell the castle to the Knight family in 1746. The castle was gothicised with money made in part from the profits of ironworks at Coalbrookdale and elsewhere in Shropshire. As a result of these changes, the castle is an important early example of the medieval revival.

The top 'storey' is simply a façade, added to impress, but so skilfully designed that it has deceived many visitors over the centuries.

The longevity of the Croft family is remarkable. Over 20 members of the Croft family have served as MPs, from the time when seats could be attained through inheritance, through to the 20th century, when election to Parliament depended upon the support of enfranchised voters. In contrast to their deeply rural seat, members of the Croft family have been involved in many key events on the national stage: fighting in the Wars of the Roses, the English Civil War and in both world wars; serving at the Courts of King Edward IV and Queen Elizabeth I; supporting refugees and artists from Nazi Germany; and serving in Churchill's war cabinet.

Below The fine *enfilade* along the south front of the house, stretching from the Oak Room, through the Blue Room and Saloon, to the Library

Croft Ambrey

There are over 2,000 hill forts in Britain and about 25 similar forts in Herefordshire. Croft Ambrey is one of only two built at more than 300 metres above sea level.

Situated on a ridge north of Croft Castle, its panoramic views explain why the site was chosen by the Celtic grain-farmers who built it around 500 BC. It was occupied for about six hundred years, possibly by the Decangi tribe. The fort's triangular-shaped plateau is defended by a steep natural drop on the north side and protected by an earth bank and ditch on the others, later extended by huge double ramparts that trace an ellipse around the hill's contour.

In 1852 the local Woolhope Naturalists' Field Club visited Croft Ambrey, led by the Scottish geologist Sir Roderick Murchison, who had published research into his discoveries at the site. In the 1960s S.C. Stanford led the Woolhope club in extensive excavations at Croft Ambrey. For years it was believed that the hill fort was a simple defensive structure, but evidence was found indicating that the interior of the fort had been occupied by Iron Age huts.

Further excavations by English Heritage in 2007 revealed that Croft Ambrey housed at least five hundred people in rows of small four-post back-to-back, single-storeyed houses lining 15-foot-wide streets. Roofs were covered with thatch, held down by limestone weights.

Underfloor space was probably used for storage, and headroom provided enough space for an upper sleeping-shelf. Water was not available on the hill-top, but would have been carried up from the spring-line just below the fort. The ramparts were extended, rectangular stone and timber guardhouses were built at both entrances and a granary building was added to store the harvest.

By the time of the Roman invasion in the 1st century AD, it had probably been abandoned. However, for centuries afterwards the fort offered such a fine defensive and commanding position that it was sometimes reused. A mound uncovered on the perimeter of the fort revealed a Romano-British shrine, with evidence of repeated fire ceremonies, animal sacrifices and feasting to have taken place for years after the Romans left.

Above Croft Ambrey from the north east with Yatton Common and Gatley Park in the distance

During the Middle Ages the ridge was used as a warren for breeding rabbits, which became an important source of food and fur. It was looked after by a warrener. As a result, the ridge has never been ploughed, leaving historical evidence intact.

In the 18th century the hill fort was incorporated into the Johnes family's Picturesque remodelling of the landscape, including paths enabling guests to use it as a picnic spot and viewing point within Fishpool Valley. There is some evidence for a summer-house in the 19th century, and an igloo-shaped ice house was added on the eastern escarpment within the valley.

Today, Croft Ambrey is a Scheduled Ancient Monument and is accessible from the castle via a waymarked path through modern conifer plantations.

Below The ditch between banks at Croft Ambrey, which covers 15 hectares (38 acres) with a main enclosure of 3.3 hectares (8½ acres)

Croft and its People

Today nothing remains of the motte-and-bailey fortification established by Bernard de Croft. A Norman Knight and founder of the Croft family, he was a descendant of the Norsemen who had lived in northern France from 911.

A 'motte' was constructed from earth, from 20–80 feet high, or could be a natural feature, or an isolated rock that might serve as a citadel. The 'bailey' was a fortified wooden enclosure, perhaps as small as 30 feet in diameter, erected on top of it. These fortifications were designed for a warrior and his small band of supporters, and were markedly different from ancient hill forts like Croft Ambrey, which served entire communities. The Domesday Book of 1086 records Bernard de Croft as settled at Croft. He is thought to have been born c.1040 so probably came from Normandy. However, he left his lands to his sons and spent his final years as a monk in the Cluniac priory of Thetford in Norfolk, while one of his sons, Jasper, participated in the taking of Jerusalem in 1100.

Left Owain Glyndŵr was the last Prince of Wales. After studying law at Westminster, he entered the service of the Earl of Arundel before a dispute over land with Lord Grey precipitated a resort to arms

The Norman Conquest did not extend to lands to the west of Croft, and under William I quasi-independent Marcher lordships became the means of containing the Welsh. This frontier society was characterised by the construction of hundreds of small castles comparable with Croft, reflecting the endemic instability of the region for almost 350 years, until Owain Glyndŵr's rebellion ended in 1409.

Croft was directly caught up in Glyndŵr's 1400 revolt through the marriage of his daughter Janet to Sir John de Croft in the 1390s. It is said that after his decisive victory over Sir Edmund Mortimer in 1402 at the Battle of Bryn Glas in Powys, Glyndŵr 'sent men to occupy Croft Ambrey as a strong defensive position'.

The Croft family crest incorporates a wounded black dragon or wyvern, which may have been created to commemorate Glyndŵr's final defeat.

During her time at Croft, Janet Glyndŵr would have mourned her brother Gruffudd, who died from bubonic plague in the Tower of London c.1412. It was there that her mother, Margaret, and two sisters also died following the fall of Glyndŵr's last stronghold, Harlech Castle, in 1409. Glyndŵr evaded capture, was never betrayed despite the offer of enormous rewards and was last seen in 1412. It has been suggested that the Prince moved between Monnington Straddle at Vowchurch and Croft Castle during his last days and that he may have died at Croft. When the base of the Turret Room in the south-east tower was excavated in 1923, there was speculation that a tall skeleton found there was that of Owain Glyndŵr.

Above The lion guarding the front door is emblematic of the Croft coat of arms

Left above The Priory of Our Lady of Thetford, founded in the early 12th century, was one of the largest monasteries in East Anglia and the burial place of the Earls and Dukes of Norfolk

Left below Built in 1283–90, Harlech Castle fell to Owain Glyndŵr in 1404 and remained his headquarters until 1409 when it surrendered after a long siege

The Tudor Crofts

The 16th-century Crofts played a prominent role in national affairs and managed to maintain the family's position through turbulent times, though sometimes more through good fortune than sound judgement.

Sir Richard Croft (d.1509)

Sir Richard is the first Croft of whom there is a likeness. His face stares out from his funerary monument in Croft Church. Beside him lies his wife, Eleanor, who was from the powerful Mortimer family of Wigmore in the same county.

In 1461 Sir Richard fought on the Yorkist side at the nearby battle of Mortimer's Cross, where the Lancastrian army led by Owen Tudor was defeated, which helped the Yorkist Edward, 4th Duke of York (whose mother was a Mortimer) towards final victory and the throne as Edward IV. Eleanor served as governess to the king's eldest son, the future Edward V, today remembered as one of the 'Princes in the Tower'.

Despite his Yorkist past and having been party to the execution of Henry VII's grandfather, Sir Richard survived the foundation of the Tudor dynasty. Henry appointed Sir Richard Treasurer of the Royal Household, a Privy Councillor and Steward to his eldest son, Prince Arthur, at Ludlow Castle, where the 15-year-old prince held court during his brief marriage to Catherine of Aragon. When Prince Arthur died from 'sweating sickness' in 1502, Sir Richard Croft accompanied the Prince's body from Ludlow Castle to Worcester Cathedral for burial.

Sir James Croft (c.1518–90)

Sir Richard's great-grandson is the first member of the family of whom there is a painted portrait. Like Sir Richard and many of his descendants, James Croft was a soldier, fighting at the siege of Boulogne in 1544, where two of his brothers were killed.

Sir James's fortunes changed for the worse with the accession of Queen Mary in 1553. He was implicated in Sir Thomas Wyatt's attempt to overthrow Mary and sent to the Tower of London, where the 20-year-old Princess Elizabeth was a fellow prisoner. Sir James Croft, undergoing brutal cross-examination soon after Wyatt's execution on 11 April, would have been aware that he might suffer a similar fate. Had Sir James provided a detailed 'confession', implicating Elizabeth in the Wyatt plot, she could have been executed.

Princess Elizabeth went on to reign over England for 44 years and she never forgot Croft's loyalty during the most perilous moment of her life. When she became queen, he was rewarded with estates in Herefordshire and Kent and made Comptroller of the Royal Household. Elizabeth also remained defiantly supportive when he fell out with many of her senior courtiers. Her chief minister, Lord Burghley, thought Croft his own worst enemy: 'the man has not the readiest way to do good to himself.' Sir James represented Herefordshire in the Commons on seven occasions from 1542 until his death, when he was buried in Westminster Abbey.

It was probably Sir James who pulled down the medieval castle, which stood to the west of the present house. It was rebuilt as a small Elizabethan mansion, constructed from bricks made on site, and more fitting for a man of Sir James's status.

Opposite The magnificent altar-tomb of Sir Richard Croft and his wife, Dame Eleanor, in St Michael's Church

Above Sir James Croft with his staff of office as Comptroller of Elizabeth I's household. He had been knighted by Edward VI in 1547

Church of St Michael and All Angels

The church predates the present castle, having been here, in some form, since at least the 12th century.

For much of the medieval period the church was also the focus of a small village, which clustered on the slope to the south and was demolished when Sir James Croft rebuilt the castle in the 1580s and improved the view by creating terraced gardens to the south.

The present church probably dates from the 14th century, was enlarged in the 15th century and remodelled in the 18th century. The small bell turret with ogee-shaped cupola was added in the late 17th century and incorporates a rare single-hand clock. In 1994 the church was re-roofed in grey Welsh slate, replacing the inappropriate red tiles put on in 1905.

Today the church serves the local parish of Yarpole. Prayers have been said in this building

by parishioners, families and the staff who lived in the castle, continuously, for at least 700 years. Many visitors enjoy its stillness and calm.

The interior is lined with Jacobean panelling of finer quality than that in the Hall of the castle. The boarded vault in the east bay was decorated in the late 17th or early 18th century with clouds and gilded stars. The nave is filled with 18th-century box pews, medieval encaustic floor tiles from workshops in Malvern and Monmouth, and a number of fine Croft family tombs dating from the early 16th century.

A chest tomb bears the effigies of Sir Richard (d. 1509) and Dame Eleanor Croft (d. 1520). Sir Richard is shown in armour with a tilting helm under his head and the heraldic Croft lion by his feet. The monument, which was created by highly skilled masons, has been moved around and reassembled during the last five centuries, but the carving is in good condition. The carving is of the highest quality and comparable to the work in Henry VII's Chapel at Westminster Abbey.

A more recent inhabitant of Croft is remembered in the stained glass of the east window: Herbert Kevill-Davies, who was killed fighting in the First World War. Two matching wall tablets side-by-side on the left-hand wall commemorate Crofts who also died in action: Sir Herbert Croft, 10th Bt, who was killed at the advanced age of 47, leading his company during the bloody landings at Gallipoli in 1915, and his son, Sir James Croft, 11th Bt, who saw action in the Norway campaign and trained with No. 1 Commando during the Second World War.

Left Box pews in the church of St Michael and All Angels

Below left Sir Herbert Croft, 10th Bt, by William Carter (1863–1939). The martial service of the Crofts dates from 1100 when Sir Jasper Croft was created a Knight of the Holy Sepulchre by Godfrey of Bouillon following the taking of Jerusalem in the First Crusade

Crofts abroad

The family's good fortune waned as two Crofts depleted their wealth and were forced to live on the Continent.

Edward Croft (d. 1601)

Sir James's son and heir, Edward, followed him into Elizabeth I's Parliament as MP for Leominster and became embroiled in complex political battles. When Sir James was arrested for alleged double-dealing in diplomatic negotiations with the Duke of Palma in 1588, Edward suspected the hand of Robert Dudley, Earl of Leicester, with whom Sir James had fallen out. When the Earl died suddenly, aged 55, on the way to Buxton to take the waters for his poor health, Edward was alleged to have plotted revenge by employing a London conjuror to cast a spell on the Earl and was charged with murder, but escaped conviction for one of the more bizarre Tudor plots.

Edward Croft was a reckless and perhaps unstable character. He spent time in prison for debt and, once released, fled to the Netherlands. He was never allowed to inherit Croft, which was put in trust for his son, Herbert.

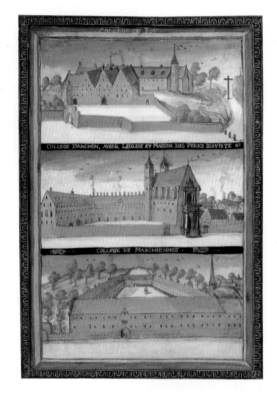

Left Illustration of the three colleges in the city of Douai painted by the prolific French topographical illustrator Adrien de Montigny

Sir Herbert Croft (1566–1629)

Herbert Croft made a good marriage to Mary Bourne, heiress of the Holt Castle estate in Worcestershire, and became one of the most prominent Parliamentarians of the early Jacobean period. He represented the local area in the Parliaments of Elizabeth I and James I, by whom he was knighted in 1603.

Herbert built the shell of the present castle in the early 17th century, and its turreted style is an early example of the romantic 'medieval revival', reflecting the Elizabethan and Jacobean nostalgia for a chivalric past, also demonstrated by sham castles at Lulworth, Dorset, and Ruperra, Glamorgan. He also created the subsequently demolished formal gardens to the south and west of the house.

In 1616 Herbert became a Catholic and the following year fled abroad to avoid his creditors. He was forced to convey part of the family estates to the Crown and wandered the Continent until 1626 when he retreated to an English Benedictine monastery at Douai in what is now the Nord département of France; since the 1560s the University of Douai had become a centre for the education of English Catholics with separate English, Welsh and Scottish colleges as well as Benedictine, Franciscan and Jesuit houses. After Herbert's death there in April 1629, he was buried at the monastery where an epitaph praises him for following the example of his 11th-century ancestor, Bernard de Croft. Herbert left behind three sons who were all destined to endure the turmoil of the Civil War.

Below Sir Herbert Croft used the turreted style of the romantic medieval revival in building the castle

The Crofts in the Civil War

In common with many country houses, Croft Castle and the family were caught up in the maelstrom of the Civil War, and ironically the castle was dismantled by the side the family had supported.

Sir William Croft (1593–1645)

After his father fled abroad, the eldest son, William, became *de facto* head of the family. He became an MP for Malmesbury in 1623 and 1625 and a Gentleman of the Privy Chamber in Prince Charles's household in 1623. He became 'a most violent man' for the Royalist cause, fighting at the Battle of Edgehill. William was caught by Parliamentary forces at Hereford in 1642 and held prisoner in Bristol for a year, until the city was retaken by the Royalist army.

In 1645, with the King's cause faltering, Sir William Croft rode to Stokesay Castle as part of a Royalist force to support its besieged owner, the Earl of Craven. After an hour's fighting, the garrison fell to Cromwell's force, leaving a hundred Royalists dead and more than 350 captured. Sir William fled on horseback and covered about 18 miles of rough roads between Stokesay and Croft Castle pursued by Parliamentarians.

Sir William reached the castle grounds, where Cromwell's musketeers shot Sir William off his horse. He collapsed against an oak tree, and died from blood loss as his family came to help him.

Right Sir William Croft's pike

The oak can still be seen from the Oak Room. In 1644 Croft Castle was ransacked by unpaid Royalist Irish levies and then dismantled to prevent it being occupied by Parliamentary troops.

Sir William was succeeded by his Royalist brother, Colonel James Croft. With the castle in ruins, he settled in London, where he died a childless bachelor in 1659. The Croft estate passed to William's youngest brother, Herbert, who was then Dean of Hereford Cathedral.

Dr Herbert Croft, Bishop of Hereford (1603–91)

Herbert Croft initially shared his father's Catholic faith, having been educated at a Jesuit college and in 1626 being admitted to the English College in Rome under an assumed name – it was a risky time to be a Catholic and publicly he conformed to the tenets of the Church of England. He began his career as Chaplain to Charles I and in 1644 he became Dean of Hereford Cathedral. During the Civil War, the cathedral was overrun by Parliamentarians, who began stripping the altars. Sir Herbert denounced this vandalism from the pulpit, and soldiers were on the point of firing their muskets when their commander intervened.

Croft survived but lost all his church posts and would have been destitute had he not succeeded to the remnants of the Croft estate. His fortunes improved with the Restoration of Charles II in 1660. He became Bishop of Hereford the following year and served the diocese for the next 30 years

'venerated… for his learning, doctrine, conversation and good hospitality'

according to a contemporary. Rather than use the grand bishop's palace in Hereford, he preferred to live mainly at Croft, which he rebuilt from his bishop's salary of £800 a year, adding a new service wing on the north side of the building.

Left Dr Herbert Croft, Bishop of Hereford, English School

Below left *Colonel Sir James Croft* (d.1659) in the manner of Michiel Jansz. van Miereveldt (1567–1641). The sash indicates that Sir James was a soldier in one of the English regiments in Dutch service

Below right Charles I by Bernard Lens III (1681–1740), after the equestrian portrait by Van Dyck

The loss of Croft

The financial losses from one of the recurrent speculative bubbles that have punctuated modern history cost the Croft family their ancestral home, at least for 150 years.

Sir Herbert Croft, 1st Bt (*c.*1652–1720)

The Bishop of Hereford's only son was created a baronet in 1671 for his family's loyal service to the Stuart cause, and four years later he married Elizabeth Archer, the sister of the gentleman-architect Thomas Archer of Umberslade in Warwickshire, who designed St John's, Smith Square in Westminster. She bore him 11 children, six of whom survived her. The line of small gilt-framed portraits in the Saloon are thought to be the 1st Baronet's children.

Sir Herbert became MP for Herefordshire in 1679, 1690 and 1695, often at odds with the Harleys of Brampton Bryan near Ludlow, before ill-health in the 1690s forced him to take the waters at Tunbridge Wells. By 1700 he was too frail to travel, and gave up his seat in Parliament, although he lived on for another 20 years.

Left Sir Herbert Croft, 1st Bt, English School

in 1720 he faced a much greater financial challenge when the South Sea Bubble burst, incurring heavy losses. The South Sea Company had been created in 1711 to consolidate and reduce the cost of the national debt, but was granted exclusive rights of trade to the Spanish Indies. The company underwrote the English National Debt, which stood at £30 million, on a promise of 5 per cent interest from the Government. Investors were seized by the same kind of irrationality that had fuelled the earlier tulip mania, causing the share price to rise from £100 in January 1720 to over £1,000 that summer.

In the inevitable crash that followed, many people throughout the country lost fortunes. Sir Archer Croft was amongst 462 members of the House of Commons and 112 Peers who had invested money in the South Sea Company and suffered in the subsequent crash. Despite retiring in 1734 with a pension of £1,000 a year, his finances never recovered and he was forced to mortgage and then in 1746 to sell the Croft estate to Richard Knight (1693–1765) of Downton Castle near Ludlow.

Left Sir Archer Croft, 2nd Bt, in a pastel by Lewis Vaslet (1742–1808)

Below *Emblematical Print on the South Sea Scheme* by William Hogarth, 1721. The scene depicts the Guildhall on the left surmounted by the statue of Gog (or Magog) and in the centre the wheel of fortune illustrating the broad section of society caught up in the collapse of the South Sea Company

Sir Archer Croft, 2nd Bt (1683–1753)

Sir Archer Croft followed his father into Parliament as MP for Leominster from 1722 and Bere Alston in Devon from 1728, and managed to ingratiate himself with Prime Minister Sir Robert Walpole, who gave him a lucrative job on the Board of Trade. In 1739 he was appointed Governor of New York, which was then a thriving port and centre of slavery, but he never visited it.

Sir Archer made extensive improvements to the gardens. A water pipe was installed to feed a fountain built into the south garden, and three terraces were added around 1700. It was probably also during his time that the windows overlooking the interior courtyard of the castle were bricked up in response to the window tax, which gave rise to the phrase 'daylight robbery'. Whether or not Sir Archer managed to save money by bricking up some of the windows,

New owners: Elizabeth Knight and Thomas Johnes I (c.1721–80)

Richard Knight's family wealth was founded upon ownership of Bringewood Ironworks in Herefordshire and later Prescott New Forge in Shropshire, and management of Moreton Forge at Moreton Mill in Coalbrookdale, the cradle of the Industrial Revolution.

Richard Knight's father, also Richard (1659–1745), had developed ironmaking interests in the Stour Valley of Worcestershire in partnership with Sir Thomas Lyttelton of Hagley Hall. The Knights went on to become the family with the longest involvement in the iron trade, from the 17th to 20th centuries.

Richard Knight bought Croft as a wedding gift for his only child and heir, Elizabeth, and her husband, Thomas Johnes (c.1721–80). In his youth Thomas Johnes had moved from the manor house at Llanfair Clydogau in Cardiganshire, where the family owned silver and lead mines, to become a leading figure in London society as well as MP for Radnorshire. None the less he seems to have lived somewhat in the shadow of his wife, Elizabeth, a strong-willed woman worth £70,000, who kept tight hold on the purse strings.

In their landscaping tastes, the Knights looked to the Picturesque. One of Richard Knight's nephews, Edward Knight, was a friend of the poet and revolutionary gardener William Shenstone, creator of the influential gardens at The Leasowes, near Halesowen, between 1743 and 1763. Richard Knight was also an admirer of Sanderson Miller, the gentleman-architect of houses and Gothick follies who was then busy building Hagley Hall in Worcestershire. Other nephews included Richard Payne Knight, who was to rebuild Downton as a mock-Gothick castle in 1774–8, and Thomas Andrew Knight, the eminent horticulturist who conducted breeding experiments with strawberries, cabbages and peas at Downton. He also bred apple trees such as the Downton Pippin, the Elton Cherry and the 'Moorpark' apricot.

When Elizabeth and her husband moved to Croft Castle, it would have appeared dated and old-fashioned, having changed little since Sir Herbert Croft's restoration a century earlier. The Johnes chose the fashionable local architect Thomas Farnolls Pritchard of Shrewsbury to remodel and update the exterior and interiors in the new rococo Gothick style made fashionable

Below Coalbrookdale landscape with Abraham Darby III's Iron Bridge of 1777–81 and one of the smaller Severn barges, used principally for carrying coal

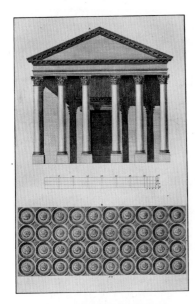

by designers such as Sanderson Miller and Batty Langley. Johnes may have been encouraged in his choice of style by his friend, John, 2nd Viscount Bateman of nearby Shobdon Court, where the parish church had been remodelled in a version of rococo Gothick in 1752–6.

Above The Saloon; Pritchard's ceiling plasterwork features octagonal coffering inspired by the illustrations of classical ceilings in Robert Wood's *Ruins of Palmyra*

Thomas Farnolls Pritchard (c.1723–77)

Pritchard is chiefly remembered as the designer of the world's first iron bridge, at Coalbrookdale in Shropshire, but his interior decorative work includes many other sites in the Marches and other National Trust houses such as Benthall Hall, Shipton Hall and Powis Castle.

Until the 1950s many of his achievements had been forgotten, but in 1964 an album of his work containing designs for Gothick doorcases and overmantels at Croft was discovered by the architectural historian John Harris in the library of the American Institute of Architects in Washington DC. The album was subsequently republished. Pritchard is now respected as a provincial designer of great individuality with an idiosyncratic flair, epitomised by his speciality of Rococo chimneypieces. Pritchard is credited with creating a fashion for the Neo-Gothic in Shropshire and Herefordshire.

Pritchard adopted the Rococo-Gothick style to remodel Croft's interior and exterior in the 1760s. One of his achievements was to bring together a band of highly skilled craftsmen to undertake the carving. These craftsmen translated his drawings into different interiors, with many collaborating on one element.

Left The east entrance front with its Gothick bay windows is largely the work of Thomas Farnolls Pritchard in the 1760s

For example, the creation of one chimneypiece took Pritchard's master craftsmen Nelson, Van Hagen and Danders about 35 days of continuous work.

Though later rearrangement has somewhat obscured Pritchard's work, his designs are evident today in the castle's entrance front, with its two pretty Gothick bays, on the staircase and in the intricate plasterwork ceilings and doorcases. The Blue Room is the most complete 18th-century room, although its elaborate chimneypiece and overmantel incorporating trophies of musical instruments came from the Oak Room. He created the Gothick staircase on the south-west side with a lightness of touch that avoided discordant notes with the classical detail of the doorcase into today's Dining Room.

Work was also carried out in the garden. At an uncertain date a heated glasshouse was installed which might have grown such fruit as pineapples and melons. Evidence of this structure can be seen from markings and the white limewash on the north wall of the walled garden. Holes at the top of the wall indicate that there was also a wall-mounted vine house facing into the garden.

Right above **Detail of the newly conserved Blue Room panelling and a Sheraton-style five-and-a half octave square piano with decorative inlay made by William Southwell in Dublin in 1784**

Detail of the Blue Room rococo chimneypiece decoration of musical instruments from the workshop of Nelson and Van Hagen of Shrewsbury

Right below **The Blue Room takes its name from the colour Pritchard chose for the Jacobean panelling he introduced in the 1760s, thought to have come from the Knight house of Stanage Park in Radnorshire**

The Gothick Staircase, designed by Pritchard whose plasterwork was obscured in the late 19th century when it was unfashionable. In the 1970s it was reinstated by sculpting and moulding the raised plaster decoration by Albert Compton

Thomas Johnes II: creating a paradise in Wales

The Johnes's eldest son, Thomas (1748–1816), was born at Dinham House in Ludlow but brought up at Croft, which may have fuelled his fascination with the Middle Ages and encouraged his translation of Froissart's *Chronicles*.

At Eton he studied Latin and Greek under William Windham of Felbrigg Hall (also National Trust) before a three-year Grand Tour of the Continent

with the Scottish diplomat Robert Liston. On their return, Thomas's father introduced him to their Welsh estates, and at Hafod in a remote valley 15 miles from Aberystwyth the younger Thomas told Liston that he had found 'Paradise'.

Before Thomas could realise his vision of creating a Picturesque landscape in the remote wilderness of mid-Wales, he was married and widowed within a year and married again, to his first cousin, Jane Johnes of Dolaucothi (also

Above Hafod House and park by Joseph Constantine Stadler (fl. 1780–1812)

National Trust). The hasty marriage, coupled with their move to Hafod, caused a severe rift in the family. However, the couple shared a love of the place and devoted their time and Thomas's inheritance to improving farming and local amenities as well as reshaping the landscape, urged on by the two most influential proponents of the Picturesque, his cousin Richard Payne Knight and friend Sir Uvedale Price.

The watercolourist George Cumberland called it 'the sweetest interchange of hill and valley, rivers, woods and plains, and falls with forest, crown'd, rocks, dens and caves'. The Hafod dairy produced Parmesan, Stilton, Gloucester and Cheshire cheeses 'so excellent in quality, and so exact in the imitation of shape and flavour, as to deceive the most accurate eye or palate.' At the heart of the estate was a house designed by Thomas Baldwin of Bath which was completed in 1788 and substantially altered from 1793 by John Nash who built an octagonal library. Johnes filled the house with beautiful objects, including paintings by Rubens, Salvatore Rosa and Van Dyck.

Thomas had over three million trees planted and laid out walks and drives so that guests could enjoy the landscape as an ever-changing sequence of views. He received the Royal Society of Arts medal for tree planting on five occasions. On display at Croft are his portrait, his bust and a collection of views of Hafod of the 1790s.

Though Johnes became MP for Cardigan in 1774 and served another eight terms for Radnorshire and Cardiganshire, he confessed that 'no one ever took less pains for a seat in Parliament than myself, and had I not been so honourably called on, I should have remained here in quiet, planting my cabbages.'

Below The East Staircase; the bust of Thomas Johnes II is surrounded by watercolours of Hafod, the landscape park in mid-Wales created by Johnes

The sale of Hafod

Eventually Thomas's spending at Hafod incurred such debts that he had to sell the Croft estate after 1799, forcing his justifiably furious mother to give up her father's wedding present to her and retire to London.

In 1807 Hafod House, whose library contained priceless collections of early Welsh and French manuscripts, burned to the ground, and in 1811 the Johnes's only child, Marianne, died.

Though underinsured, the house was rebuilt by Thomas Baldwin and furnished with many items bought from the sale of Beckford's Fonthill Splendens. Heavy debts and progressive mortgages compounded Johnes's financial plight, and after an illness he and his wife retired to Langstone Cliff Cottage near Dawlish in Devon, where he died in 1816. He is buried at Eglwys Newydd, the church designed by James Wyatt for Johnes at Hafod.

After a lengthy wrangle in the Court of Chancery, exemplified by the fictitious Jarndyce and Jarndyce in Dickens's *Bleak House*, the 4th Duke of Newcastle took over Hafod in 1833. A huge extension by Anthony Salvin in the late 1840s made it unmanageable, and a century later it was empty and dilapidated. It was finally blown up in 1958. Today the estate of Hafod is recognised as one of the finest examples in Europe of a Picturesque landscape and is being restored by Natural Resources Wales, in partnership with the Hafod Trust.

Works from Johnes's Hafod Press, the first private press in Wales, are on display in the Library at Croft; the press published mainly translations from French chronicles and some travel journals.

At Croft, Johnes is credited with the addition of the gate, tower and curtain wall which visitors pass through on their way to the castle, as well as the avenue and the battlemented terrace. His preference for landscaping rather than formal gardens resulted in the removal of terraced gardens to the south of the castle. The present sash-windows were installed at this time, replacing earlier, smaller ones. The new windows were designed to frame the Johnes's now fashionably landscaped park and the distant views it afforded. The present stable block was also added, and though the horse stalls have been converted into the Stables shop and secondhand book-shop, some of the 20th-century loose boxes for the family's hunters still remain.

Right A marble bust of Thomas Johnes II, ordered in 1811 at a cost of £105

Right The eight Library bookcases were designed in the 1760s and contain books owned by the Croft Trust, many of them by or associated with members of the family. The brass 'trellis' was added in the 20th century

The Crofts in Exile

The Croft baronets of the later 18th and 19th centuries may have been separated from their ancestral home, but their stories and activities are reflected in many artefacts and pictures at Croft today.

Left The Blue Room with Gainsborough's portrait of Elizabeth Cowper, wife of the 3rd Baronet, over the mantelpiece

The 3rd and 4th Baronets

After the sale of Croft to the Knight family, the 3rd Baronet, another Archer (1731–92), moved from Croft to his mother's family home, Dunston Park in Berkshire (now demolished). In 1759 he married a cousin of the poet William Cowper, the renowned beauty Elizabeth Cowper, whose portrait by Thomas Gainsborough is displayed at Croft. She was also painted by Gainsborough's great rival, Sir Joshua Reynolds. The couple's son died young, so on Archer's death in 1792, the title passed to his bachelor brother John, briefly the 4th Baronet, and then on to a cousin.

Rev. Sir Herbert Croft, 5th Bt (1751–1816)

Born at Dunston Park, Herbert Croft matriculated at University College, Oxford, and trained as a lawyer at Lincoln's Inn. Called to the bar in 1775 he practised at Westminster Hall but, given his later financial difficulties, unwisely abandoned the law to return to University College to study for holy orders. Though given the vicarage of Prittlewell in Essex, he chose to remain in Oxford where he devoted years to revising Samuel Johnson's *Dictionary of English Language*, originally published in 1755. By 1790 he had assembled 11,000 words missing from it, and his notes on it filled 200 quarto volumes. He proposed to publish a new dictionary in 1792, but without sufficient subscriptions he had to abandon the costly project (Johnson's original dictionary sold 2,000 copies, but had cost several months' average income). A copy of Dr Johnson's dictionary with annotations by Herbert is on display.

He wrote books and articles on many subjects, even a bestselling book based on the murder in Covent Garden of the actress Martha Rae, mistress of the Earl of Sandwich, by her besotted lover James Hackman. But his reputation was indelibly stained by the revelation of the circumstances in which he obtained and profited from letters which had belonged to the poet Thomas Chatterton. The 18-year-old had committed suicide in 1770, and Herbert had obtained the letters from the poet's wife and sister under false pretences and used them without consent.

Herbert was a poor manager of his finances: the day after his second marriage he was put in Exeter prison for debt. Upon his release he retired to Hamburg and spent most of the rest of his life in exile in Lille and Amiens, in a château owned by his friend the novelist Lady Mary Hamilton, and in Paris. There was a brief interlude during 1800–2 in Southend from where he discharged his duties as vicar to Prittlewell. He had inherited the title of Baronet in 1797, but it made little difference, as the Croft Estate was not his, and when Sir Herbert died the title was passed down to his younger brother, one of the leading obstetricians of Regency London.

Below left *The Rev. Sir Herbert Croft, 5th Bt, with a bust of Samuel Johnson,* by Lemuel Francis Abbott (1760–1803)

Below right Dr Johnson's Dictionary, annotated by Sir Herbert Croft

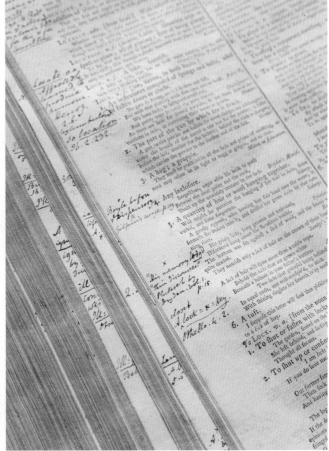

A national controversy

Sir Richard Croft, 6th Bt (1762–1818) received his medical education at St Bartholomew's Hospital in London and Aberdeen before taking up a position at Tutbury in Staffordshire.

A letter of introduction to the distinguished physician Thomas Denman, led to Richard marrying his daughter Margaret, as well as absorbing his father-in-law's ideas on minimal intervention in the course of labour. Some of Thomas Denman's works on midwifery are found in the Library. Richard became one of London's leading obstetricians, having made his name after attending the Duchess of Devonshire at the birth of her son in 1790. The year after succeeding to the baronetcy in 1816, Sir Richard was appointed Surgeon-in-Ordinary to the Prince of Wales and Prince Leopold. Leopold was married to the Prince of Wales's only legitimate child, Charlotte, who was as popular as her father was unpopular. They lived at Claremont in Surrey, where the landscape garden is in the care of the National Trust. Princess Charlotte began her pregnancy as a healthy young woman, but was weakened after months of blood-letting and a strict diet prescribed by Sir Richard. After a ghastly 52-hour labour, a 9lb baby boy was still-born. Had the baby lived, he would have become king and there would have been no Queen Victoria, no Kaiser Wilhelm II and no haemophilia in the Russian royal family. The baby had been breech, but Sir Richard and another adviser followed the practice of non-intervention, although many thought a forceps delivery should have been attempted.

Charlotte seemed at first to have survived, but she began to haemorrhage and died the following day. Her death generated a national outpouring of grief, summed up by Byron:

…in the dust
The fair-haired daughter of the Isles is laid,
The love of millions, how we did entrust
Futurity to her…

Sir Richard became the victim of a media witch-hunt that blamed him for her death, and there were calls for a public inquiry. Croft was distraught at the outcome of the pregnancy and deeply affected by the public criticism.

A necropsy ordered by the king placed no blame on Sir Richard, who received sympathy from the royal family and many of his profession. He returned to practice but was never able to overcome the depression that had set in, and he appeared to have lost all self-confidence. While attending a birth in Wimpole Street, he shot himself with two pistols at the age of 56 in an upper room assigned for his use. Sir Thomas Lawrence was commissioned by the family to make a posthumous sketch of Sir Richard in his coffin, which hangs at Croft.

Below left *The Children of Sir Richard Croft, 6th Bt* by John James Halls (1776–1853), *c*.1803. The children are (from left to right) Archer (1801–65), Frances (1800–77), Thomas (1798–1835) and, at the back with a book, Herbert (1793–1803). Thomas holds a delicate china cup and blows a soap bubble from a clay pipe – both symbols of the fragility of young life. The references seem to have been personal, as there is a family tradition that the portrait of Herbert, who sits apart dressed in black, was painted posthumously. There are memorial tablets to Herbert and Thomas on the outside west wall of St James's Church, Piccadilly

Below right *Sir Richard Croft, 6th Bt*, in the posthumous portrait by Sir Thomas Lawrence (1769–1830)

Croft Castle in the Victorian and Edwardian era

In or soon after 1799 Thomas Johnes sold the Croft estate for £56,000 to Somerset Davies (c.1754–1817) who owned nearby Wigmore Hall, also remodelled by T.F. Pritchard, an estate at Wellington and land and property in Kingsland, Lucton, Aston and the Mortimer's Cross Mill.

Originating from the county of the same name, the Somerset Davies family were prosperous Ludlow mercers dealing in wool, velvets and silks. The 18th-century Enclosure Acts and the expanding property and land market saw Davies actively buying and selling land and leases, and granting loans and mortgages. Gaining wealth and status in Shropshire and Herefordshire, Davies served as a JP and MP. His daughter Anne Isabella married James Kevill, a clergyman from Cornwall and lived at Croft.

Somerset Davies added the 'Gothic Arch' straddling the castle drive as part of the fake-medieval curtain wall added about 1810. During this time the walled garden was extensively cultivated and gradually formalised. The formal gardens once extended to 2½ acres beyond the west wall with wide herbaceous border, geometric rose beds and a glass conservatory for tender plants. A terrace was added in time for a dance held for Anne in 1804.

Edward, the eldest son of James and Anne, died before his majority so the castle and estate were inherited in 1847 by their second son, the Rev. William Trevelyan Somerset Kevill (1826–1906). In accordance with his grandfather's will, the name Kevill-Davies was adopted. Alterations made by William to Croft Castle do not seem to have been recorded but photographs from the early 1900s show a comfortable Edwardian country house. William and his wife, Ellen, had nine children. The eldest, also William, had a noted military career in the 7th Hussars, including service in the Zulu Wars. Posted to Dublin, he married Lily Armstrong and his children were born there. Moving back to Croft, William succumbed to poor health and died in 1896.

In 1906 his son William Albert Somerset Herbert inherited Croft from his grandfather, having also enjoyed a distinguished career in the 7th Hussars, receiving the Queens Medal for service in the Boer War. In 1908 he married Dorothy Matlock de Montesquoi Lacon, heiress to the Great Yarmouth Lacon brewery, and the couple returned to Croft where their three sons were born. It appears the family preferred to live at Highwood, a large white house on the estate, renting out the castle to first Lord Justice Holmes and then Major Evelyn Atherley.

Herbert rejoined his regiment at the outbreak of the First World War and while attached to the 9th Lancers died of wounds on 15 May 1915 at the 2nd Battle of Ypres, aged 38. He is buried in France at the Commonwealth War Graves Cemetery at Bailleul. The original grave marker brought back to Croft Church, reputedly by Owen Croft, can be seen there today. Dorothy installed the east window to his memory and family memorials in Yarpole Church.

Opposite, clockwise from top left The Gothic arch built into the earlier curtain wall by Somerset Davies c.1810

Herbert Kevill-Davies (on the left) in the trenches, 1915

The walled garden with the north front of the castle beyond. The garden today looks very different from its period of intensive cultivatation by the Somerset Davies family

Herbert Kevill-Davies

The servants

Before the mechanisation of many household tasks and the installation of central heating, country houses could not function without a large number of servants.

The 1861 census lists the following servants working and living at Croft Castle: 2 governesses, 3 nurses, a head housemaid, an upper laundress, second laundress, 2 kitchen maids, housemaid, dairymaid, housekeeper, lady's maid, a butler, footman, coachman and groom. These 18 staff were employed to look after the 11 listed members of the Kevill-Davies family. The governesses came from London and Norfolk, while the other staff are listed as having been born in Buckinghamshire, Lincolnshire, Nottinghamshire and Yorkshire. Others were born locally, in Herefordshire, Worcestershire and Shropshire.

   During the occupation of Croft by the Johnes family, it was customary for gentleman and ladies to separate after dinner. The men would retire to the Oak Room, and ladies would be entertained in the Blue Room.

   Before cess pits were made at the castle, most waste would be recycled as fertiliser on vegetable plots. However, by the 19th century Croft's staff had the luxury of access to a toilet block in the servants' courtyard, which is today just beyond the Secret Garden. They may also have been able to wash in the laundry which was housed inside the servants' wing.

Margaret Powell, a former servant who also worked in London and died in 1984, recalled in her memoirs:

'I shared with another maid and the room was so cold in winter that the ice froze in the jugs of water we used for washing.'

From the upstairs gallery at Croft, looking across the courtyard to the north wing, you can see four windows of the attic room. After the servants' quarters were demolished in 1937, this room was used to house the remaining staff.

   Labour-saving devices and rising wages in alternative sources of employment gradually reduced the huge servant class. When the 1891 census was taken, the number of servants at Croft had been reduced to just four, though this undoubtedly reflected the financial constraints of the Kevill-Davies family. They moved into Highwood House on the estate, which they retained until 1948, and let Croft to their friends, the Atherleys.

Above The servants *c.*1901

Opposite Poster advertising the building materials salvaged from the demolitions of 1937

CROFT CASTLE

HEREFORDSHIRE
6 miles from Leominster.
Important Demolition Sale.

JOHN NORTON

is favoured with instructions from the Contractors (Messrs. TURFORD & SOUTHWARD, Ltd.)
to Sell by Auction

On SATURDAY, 19th JUNE, 1937

the whole of the Valuable

BUILDING MATERIALS

in consequence of a wing of the mansion being dismantled, including a large quantity of
OAK and other BEAMS, chiefly moulded faces, in good average lengths—28 feet and upwards,

SOUND OAK and other SQUARE-EDGED FLOORING BOARDS

carefully taken up, with the original polishing preserved.

A large quantity of Oak Sawn Square Timber from Floor-joists, Ceilings, Roof,
Half-Timbering, &c., Oak Window Frames,
Adjustable Oak and Iron Glazed Leaded Casements,

A large number of OAK DOORS, various sizes

with furnishings complete.

Two Flights of Period Stairs,

in various woods, with pleasing balustrades,

A large assortment of Fire Grates and Mantels

Cupboards and Fittings, Radiators,

Hand-made Bricks, Slates, Sanitary Fittings,

Stacks of Firewood, Sawn Timber, Taper Baths, Sinks, Quarries,
Scrap Metal and numerous other effects (300 lots).

Sale to commence at 12-30 o'clock.

VIEW DAYS—Thursday and Friday, June 17th and 18th, from 10-30 until 5 o'clock.

Full particulars may be obtained from the Contractors—Messrs. TURFORD & SOUTHWARD Ltd. Ludlow

Left The Tudor-style
panelling in the Hall was
introduced by Walter Sarel

Major Atherley and Walter Sarel

The castle was leased in 1913 to Major Evelyn Atherley (1852–1935) of the Horse Guards. He invested a great deal of his own money to modernise the house, commissioning the architect Walter Sarel, who designed houses in the Arts and Crafts style and worked with Gertrude Jekyll.

He carried out external alterations by simplifying the roof line and toning down some of Pritchard's spikier Gothick decoration. Some of his work at Croft was practical, conserving heat through the addition of an entrance porch, along with the installation of a plain stone fireplace and Tudor-style panelling in the Hall. The Atherleys installed central heating in ground-floor rooms, corridors and one room on the first floor, the Ambassador's Room. Their radiators are still in use. They also installed four grand bathrooms, three of which were dismantled and reverted to bedrooms, and an upstairs kitchen.

To reduce the distance from kitchen to dining-table, the Dining Room was relocated and the room remodelled in an 18th-century style. Sarel installed a Venetian window from another part of the house and inserted a screen of Ionic columns – an 18th-century feature used to separate the diners from the serving area. He also moved two pieces of carving by Pritchard from the Library, and installed them over the chimney and sideboard. Their designs, of the vases of flowers and swags, are contained in the album of Pritchard's work in the Library of Congress in Washington. Sarel moved

Pritchard's elaborate limewood chimneypiece and overmantel from the Oak Room to the Blue Room.

In 1913 Major Atherley installed an earlier glasshouse of 1908 by J. Weeks & Co., botanical engineers of London, in the walled garden; this fell into disrepair but is currently being restored by the National Trust. Since 2008 every pane of glass has been removed and metal work repainted; original ironwork 'staging' for the plants has now been reinstated, and plants grown here are sold by the gardeners to fund conservation work in the garden.

Above The Dining Room was created from the west hall in 1913 by Walter Sarel who used Pritchard's carving from the Library over the chimneypiece and sideboard

Below left The glasshouse installed by Major Atherley was made by J. Weeks & Co. in King's Road, London

The Crofts Return

The 6th Baronet's grandson, Sir Herbert Croft, 9th Bt (1838–1902), began the Croft family's gradual return to their ancestral home by settling at Lugwardine Court near Hereford and serving as MP for the area from 1868 to 1874.

His son and heir, another Herbert, was commissioned into the Herefordshire Regiment at the advanced age of 46 on the outbreak of the First World War in 1914. A year later he was killed leading his company during the bloody landings that opened the disastrous Gallipoli campaign, leaving behind a widow, the infant 11th Baronet, Sir James Croft (1907–41), and his sister, Elinor.

In 1923 the Trustees of Sir James Croft were able to buy back the castle after a gap of more than 170 years. Portraits can be found in the castle of Sir James and his sister Elinor, who moved into the castle from Lugwardine together with their mother Katherine when the castle was purchased. The family supported the Ludlow Hunt, and in 1930 held the Ludlow Hunt Ball at the castle, with 250 guests.

To make the castle more practical, the Trustees demolished the old service wing in 1937. But holding on to Croft during the following years of war and austerity was to prove difficult and complex. During the Second World War, Sir James fought in the Norway Campaign in which the Allies helped Norway to hold out for 62 days against invasion by Germany. Sir James was then stationed in Scotland, where he was killed in 1941 while training with No. 1 Commando. Sir James is buried in Fishpool Valley. The baronetcy is now held by Sir Owen Croft, 14th Bt, who lives in New South Wales.

Below Sir Herbert George Denman Croft, 9th Bt, as a boy by Carl Hartman (1818–57)

The childless Sir James had already bequeathed Croft to his cousin, Brigadier-General Sir Henry Page Croft, 1st Lord Croft, because he thought that Lord Croft, who had married an heiress, would have the money to maintain the estate. He had his own inheritance from the family business in East Anglian grain and malt. However, Sir James omitted to tell his cousin of his intentions.

Above left *Sir James Croft, 11th Bt* by James P. Barraclough (fl. 1925–42)

Above right *Belinda at Croft* by James P. Barraclough, 1927. Sir James Croft's sister Elinor was known as 'Belinda' and she was depicted in the upstairs corridor at the top of the Gothick Stairs

A land girl's memory of Croft

'I joined the Women's Land Army in March 1942… My destination was Leominster in Herefordshire, we had never heard of the place, never having been any further than Scarborough or Bridlington. We had a girl from London, Stepney, she worried about her family in the Blitz, she was called Louise… One job I went on with Lou was to Croft Castle, to do some gardening for a Mrs Parr, her brother owned the castle which was taken over by a school. Mrs Parr lived in the lodge, we cycled up the long drive, it was a lovely place, there were red squirrels darting about in the trees, she wanted potatoes planting etc., there was a lot of digging to do. After a while Lou said to me, slow down Mitzi, only fools and horses work. It was the first time I'd heard that expression…'

Sir Henry Page Croft,
1st Lord Croft (1881–1947)

The Croft estate was at its lowest ebb when in 1941, upon the death of his cousin Sir James in Scotland, Brigadier-General Sir Henry Croft heard the surprising news that he had inherited Croft Castle. At the time, he was Under-Secretary for War in Churchill's wartime government and approaching the end of a long and turbulent political career.

During the First World War, Sir Henry had served with great distinction, commanding a brigade in the Battle of the Somme. However, he was persuaded that he could better serve the war effort by returning to Parliament, and in 1917 he helped to found the independent National Party, which worked to preserve the British Empire.

He married the Hon. Nancy Borwick, whose fortune came from her family's baking powder company. Their portraits, painted by the fashionable artist Philip de László, are displayed in the Dining Room. Throughout the inter-war years, Sir Henry kept his Bournemouth seat as an Independent, and then as a Tory, supporting Churchill's campaign for rearming and against Indian self-government. He campaigned for the creation of 'homes fit for heroes' and for an end to the sale of honours.

Right *Henry, 1st Lord Croft* by Philip de László (1869–1937), 1929; Dining Room

During the Second World War the castle was occupied by St Mary's convent school, evacuated from Hereford. At Croft, the nuns would put disobedient children into the south-west tower's Turret Room. It is not clear whether the tower would have been lit when the children were put in it, but it is unlikely to have been heated.

While serving in Churchill's wartime government, Sir Henry encouraged the security services, MI5 and MI6, to work together in support of the war effort. However, in a speech about resistance following a German invasion, his suggestion that pikes might come in handy after hand grenades had been thrown at the enemy was satirised in an Illingworth cartoon, a copy of which is in the castle.

In 1946 when the school left, the staff at Croft laid on a welcome home party for Sir Henry, now Lord Croft, who was finally able to return to his inheritance of the castle and just 35 acres. He began the urgent task of renewing all the slate and leadwork on the roof and reviving the shabby decoration, but died the following year before he could complete it.

Left *Nancy, 1st Lady Croft* by Philip de László (1869–1937), 1924; Dining Room

Michael, 2nd Lord Croft and Diana Uhlman

Michael Croft, who became the 2nd Lord Croft, had already bought back the remainder of the historic estate in 1942, but the inheritance of his father's estate in 1947 put Croft in jeopardy.

Faced with crippling death duties, the castle was first sold to a cousin, Major Owen Croft (1880–1956), the family's historian, in the hope that he would have the money to run it. Though Major Croft was not wealthy, he was able to buy Croft thanks to his wife Stella, an Argentinian heiress whose wealth derived from her stepfather, Cardwell Brown of Ludford Park, Ludlow. His fortune was made from wool, beef and railways during the last quarter of the 19th century. After Major Croft's death in 1956, his widow Stella put Croft up for sale.

Fearful that the house might be demolished if it were sold, Michael Croft and his sister Diana Uhlman were instrumental in saving Croft, refurbishing the castle and restoring the estate. Lord Croft's second great interest was British contemporary art, and through his sister and her husband was able to make valuable connections with émigré artists, long before they were to achieve recognition. Through them he met Oskar Kokoschka and commissioned a portrait. Lord Croft also provided the *South West View of the Castle* by John Napper and *East Front of Croft Castle* by Kenneth Rowntree. His collection eventually included works by Picasso, Ben Nicholson, Barbara Hepworth, David Hockney,

In 1933 Fred Uhlman had been a successful young lawyer in Stuttgart and was an active member of the Social Democratic Party. The rise of the Nazi party put him in danger of arrest and he fled to Paris, where, unable to practise law, he became a painter. In 1936 he moved to Spain and after his marriage to Diana Croft, the couple returned to live in Chelsea and then Hampstead, where their home became a favourite cultural and artistic meeting place for refugees. Fred founded the Free German League of Culture with Oscar Kokoschka and the writer Stefan Zweig. In 1940, along with hundreds of other anti-Nazi German Jews, Uhlman was interned on the Isle of Man. This experience affected him deeply but enriched him artistically.

Opposite The portrait of 2nd Lord Croft by Oskar Kokoschka (1886–1980), whose outspoken opposition to the Nazis led to his move to England in 1938

Left Michael Henry Glendower Page Croft, 2nd Baron Croft in front of the Library Ante-room fireplace, by John Napper (1916–2001), 1987

Below Michael and Diana Uhlman

Henry Moore, Jasper Johns, Bridget Riley and many other key figures of 20th-century art. Lord Croft was an honorary keeper of the Fitzwilliam Museum in Cambridge, to which he left works by Paul Nash and eight beautiful watercolours by Kokoschka on his death in 1997 when most of his collection was sold.

Diana Uhlman married the German artist and writer Fred Uhlman, whom she had met on Spain's Costa Brava in 1936, much against her more conservative parents' wishes. However, it was a union of opposites which lasted for nearly fifty years.

Saving Croft

Croft was saved through the combined efforts of several different parties: the National Land Fund, which had been set up to honour the memory of the war dead (two members of the Croft family among them), the National Trust and, equally importantly, members of the Croft family – Michael, 2nd Lord Croft, Mrs Owen Croft and Diana Uhlman.

Lord Croft's sister, Diana Uhlman, led the campaign, rallying the support of Christopher Hussey, the influential architectural editor of *Country Life*. Lord Croft endowed the castle, supported by Diana Uhlman and Edward Croft-Murray along with a public appeal. The family provided furniture, carpets, curtains, chandeliers and many family portraits. Diana Uhlman also encouraged her brother to take up residence and to create apartments that were made available to other family members.

The collection at Croft has largely been created since the mid-20th century when members of the family supported the transfer of the castle and sought to decorate and furnish it with objects associated with, or relevant to, the Croft and Knight families. For instance, Diana Uhlman bought the set of Hafod prints and the fine set of six Gothick chairs displayed in the Gallery.

To support the refurbishment of Croft, in 1960 Diana Uhlman established the Croft Trust as a repository for family chattels, which acquires or encourages the loan of furniture, pictures and possessions from distant family members to the National Trust, such as the portrait of Elizabeth Cowper by Thomas Gainsborough in the Blue Room.

One of the reasons for the limited number of rooms open to visitors on the first floor at Croft is the existence of two family apartments, one occupied by the 3rd Lord and Lady Croft, the other by Fred and Diana Uhlman's daughter, Mrs Caroline Compton. The present-day residence of the apartments maintains a family presence that stretches back a millennium to their namesake, Bernard de Croft.

Below Until the 1913 alterations, the Oak Room created by Thomas Farnolls Pritchard was the 'dining parlour'. The majority of the 20th-century pictures are hung in this room

Opposite Drypoint etching of Nancy, Lady Croft which is now on display in the Dining Room, thanks to the Croft Trust

The Estate and Gardens

The beauty of the estate and the significance of Croft Ambrey influenced the decision by the National Trust to take on the property in 1957.

But the walled garden in particular was in a state of disrepair, and it was preserved largely through the efforts and generosity of the Uhlmans and their daughter, Caroline Compton.

The gardens that supported earlier versions of the castle would have been functional and included vegetable and herb gardens in rectangular plots for culinary and medicinal use.

Above The walled garden, which was resurrected from the late 1950s. It was completely redesigned with dwarf stone walls, rose beds intersected with paths, herbaceous borders, an avenue of clipped Irish junipers, a beech hedge and a vineyard in the 1970s by Diana Uhlman and her volunteers

Above The bug hotel in the walled garden

Below The small vineyard in the walled garden

In the 16th century, when Sir James Croft is believed to have built the fortified Elizabethan manor house, terraced gardens were added to the south and west of the present house. When the manor was rebuilt by Dr Herbert Croft, Bishop of Hereford, the formal gardens were improved through the installation of elm pipes to supply water. The terraced gardens were removed by the Johnes family, who, in pursuit of the 18th-century preference for a Picturesque effect, levelled them to ensure that the front of the house enjoyed clear views to Hay Bluff in the south west.

The 3½-acre walled kitchen garden was created at this time. Its north wall includes the former Gardener's Cottage, which had a small formal and herb garden in front. Attached to the wall was a series of greenhouses heated from a boiler in a bothy behind. Evidence of this earlier glasshouse can be seen from markings on the north wall of the present gardens, the layout of the garden path and the white limewash. Holes at the top of the wall indicate that there could have been a wall-mounted vine house facing into the walled garden.

The walled garden was leased from 1946 to 1951 to the Croft family gardener, Fred Langridge, who sold its produce at Leominster market. Thanks to the work of Diana Uhlman, her daughter Caroline Compton, their loyal gardener and the National Trust's professional and volunteer gardening team, Croft Castle now has a walled garden that delights visitors. Diana Uhlman wanted to reflect the Picturesque movement. She also worked closely with Elizabeth Banks from Hergest Croft Gardens, also in Herefordshire, on the North Forecourt Garden, though most of the original planting has since been changed. Today the garden's walls enclose gently sloping lawns dotted with unusual apple trees and clipped Irish junipers.

The overall effect is not particularly formal, reflecting the Picturesque theme of the surrounding landscaped grounds. The small vineyard created in 1979 was moved and replanted in 2001 by Caroline Compton, with Phoenix vines more suited to northern climates. The vineyard now produces a white table wine, sold in the Stables shop. Management of the Walled Garden was taken over by the National Trust in 2011.

The castle is surrounded by simple borders. The planting on the border from the arch, around the castle and the small 'Secret Garden' was supervised by the National Trust's Garden advisor, Graham Stuart Thomas, who helped staff to preserve the garden's character with the minimum amount of maintenance. A small box-hedged garden sits next to the wall of the former Servants' Yard garden which was originally the servants' courtyard. It had a cobbled area with drainage, posts for washing lines, a toilet block and access to the laundry.

Avenues and trees

Croft's avenues are its great glories, and it is thought some of them date from Elizabethan times and formed part of the earliest designed landscape around the castle.

The Spanish Chestnut Avenue

Many of the Spanish Sweet Chestnuts are over 450 years old and run for about half a mile from the west front in a westerly direction, arranged in single and then triple lines. Local legend has it that Sir James Croft, MP for Herefordshire, took the chestnuts from a Spanish shipwreck on the Welsh coast. There is an apochryphal story that, echoing the national mood of celebration following the victory against the Spanish, Sir James planted them to replicate the crescent-shaped battle formation of the Armada. The crescent was designed to defend the Armada's weaker, heavier ships and was broken up by English fireships when the Spanish anchored off Calais. This action sealed the Armada's fate. Even today, if viewed from above, the chestnuts form a crescent, though black ink disease is slowly killing some.

The Oak Avenue Drive

This runs roughly parallel to, and just to the north of, the entrance drive. The oaks were already being celebrated in a guide published in 1808, and today some have a girth of over 8 metres. A number of oak trees are also scattered around the Spanish Chestnut crescent.

Individual trees

The oldest tree is the Quarry Oak which is estimated to have started life at roughly the same time that Bernard de Croft arrived, nearly 1,000 years ago. This grand old oak has survived partly because it is now sheltered by a quarry face. Fortunately for the oak, the quarrymen who cut the stone when it was a youngster of about 500 years old chose not to cut it down. Today the oak is 17 metres in girth. Nearby is 'Sir William's Oak' – this is the tree beneath which Sir William Croft is believed to have died within sight of his home, after being shot by Cromwell's troops.

At the far western end of the grounds, along the ancient tree walk, is a small orchard of hawthorns. It is unusual to manage hawthorns through pollarding, and it was recently found that these hawthorns were nurtured here so that the young hawthorn whips could have medlar fruit trees grafted onto them. The use of hawthorns in this way is unique, and hawthorn orchards are extremely rare.

Two Californian sequoia trees can be seen to the west of the castle; their seeds were thought to have been brought to Croft from Russia in 1943.

Below left to right The Chestnut Avenue of Spanish Chestnuts

A Spanish Chestnut planted between 1670 and 1700

Some of the sweet chestnuts at Croft are over 450 years old

The avenue of oak and beech lining the main drive. Thomas Johnes was influenced in the design of the pleasure grounds and park at Croft by works on the Picturesque by Uvedale Price and Johnes's cousin Richard Payne Knight

The wider estate

In 1925 the Forestry Commission was granted a lease of 198 years over 474 acres (192ha), to be planted with conifers. Since 2010–11 the Trust has been working in partnership with the Forestry Commission to restore areas of coniferous woodland back to historic wood pasture, which will improve biodiversity and revive many of the veteran trees found within the wood.

The current estate of about 644 hectares (1,591 acres) is part of what was once a much larger estate and features a variety of landscapes – from prehistoric field systems to ancient avenues. It encompasses historic parkland around the castle, historic pasture woodlands, traditional orchards, grassland, bracken, ponds, gardens and extensive areas of farmland. Large numbers of veteran trees support wood-decay invertebrates, fungus and lichen communities, and some of the trees are exceptionally large, including an oak with a girth of over 8.8 metres (39 feet) and a sweet chestnut over 9 metres (29½ feet) in girth.

At least ten species of bat have been detected on the estate, including the UK Biodiversity Action Plan (BAP) Priority Listed lesser horseshoe and barbastelle, and species known to roost in buildings including the BAP Priority Listed brown long-eared. Notable birds include the red-breasted and spotted flycatcher, lesser spotted and green woodpeckers, willow and marsh tits, stock dove, redstart and pied flycatcher.

Among the ponds across the estate, at least two have been known to support the protected great crested newt.

Home Farm

This farm is looked after by the Pritchard family, who have been tenant farmers here since 1944. The wood pasture within the farm has so many of the ancient trees that they have to be protected from the cattle herd. The farmland includes well-structured hedges of value to wildlife and nesting birds in particular, and the farm's weedy areas support a high density of field pansy and other common arable plants.

Reviving the Picturesque in Fishpool Valley

This valley comprises a deeply incised coombe or side valley separating Bircher Common from the estate parkland, and its small stream was dammed in a number of places to create a flight of ponds.

Fishpool Valley was originally landscaped by Thomas Johnes II in the late 18th and possibly early 19th centuries, and the gorge has similarities with the work on his estate at Hafod near Aberystwyth. Recent archaeological studies have identified different tiers of carriageways that follow the contours of the slope; these were designed to afford different perspectives of the estate. The rides enabled women, who in the 18th century had more limited access to the outdoors, to become immersed in nature. The ladies would have been able to stop off at the grotto for a picnic while their husbands might use it for fishing and drinking. The grotto was originally built as a folly and was still in use up to the early 20th century but is now thick with wild garlic.

The gorge is often 5 degrees cooler than the less enclosed landscape and offers different vistas according to the changing seasons. On one hill a 'beech hangar' (sloping woodland) was planted and provides a varied display of colour in the autumn.

There is a history of light industry in the valley, which includes a wood-fired lime kiln, quarries and charcoal-burning platforms. Limestone would have been fed into the kiln, burned and used to produce quick lime which could be used as a fertiliser or for mortar in construction.

A Gothic pump house which fed water up to the castle was advanced for its time. Water descending a pipe into the pump house powered the supply of water back up to the castle. An ice house was installed in Fishpool Valley, taking advantage of its cooler year-round temperatures; the ruins can be found to the side of a gently rising path just north of the two lower pools. The domed cellar was filled with ice in winter to help keep food fresh before the development of refrigeration in the early 20th century.

Left The Gothic-windowed gardener's cottage in the walled garden

When the National Trust first took over Croft in 1957, the focus was upon restoring the house and the walled garden. The Fishpool Valley is now registered as a Site of Special Scientific Interest and home to the protected native white-clawed crayfish in the valley ponds. The damp humid environment of the valley supports a wealth of wildlife from fallow deer to bats, woodcock and rare fritillary butterflies. A Douglas fir planted here in the early 19th century is now 65.6 metres (215 feet) tall, the third highest in England.

In 2017 the Trust was able to begin restoring the Fishpool Valley back to its Picturesque origins thanks to funds raised by supporters. The large project aims to restore the dams and pools and reinstate the lost views and architectural features and some of the original carriage rides of the valley for visitors to experience this pleasure ground as it was intended. Repairs to the structures will be largely carried out with traditional materials, including lime mortar which requires warmer temperatures.

Above The old pump house in Fishpool Valley, subject of a major restoration programme

Restoring historic wood pasture

When the Forestry Commission took a 198-year lease in 1925 on the large area of woodland which sits between the farmland and Croft Ambrey, it planted dense and fast-growing conifers around the hill fort on an area of historic wood pasture and native broadleaf trees grazed by cattle, sheep and deer.

In 2014 a partnership agreement was formed between the Forestry Commission and the National Trust to reclaim and restore a large area of the conifer woodland back to its intended and former state of historic wood pasture.

Under the guidance of Natural England and external advisory bodies, the Forestry Commission extracted a large area of conifer woodland, and the National Trust continues on a revolving lease to restore the area to grazing pasture. This comprises native broadleaf trees set amongst natural grasslands and herbs, grazed by introduced cattle which would have originally grazed here.

The conifers also blocked views to and from Croft Ambrey, the Iron Age hill fort. The National Trust ranger and his team of volunteers are clearing out the overgrowth that obscures some of the rampart systems of the hill fort itself and replacing felled conifers with broadleafed tree species, including sweet chestnut, beech and oak in areas of the wood pasture designated for replanting. In addition to improving the native planting schemes and reinstating the historic wood pasture, the countryside team are also aiming to improve the wildlife habitat and conditions along the naturally occurring water corridors within the woodland.

Thinning of the woodland growth that blocks light along the water corridor will help the dominant mixture of meadowsweet and opposite-leaved golden-saxifrage, with frequent wood sedge, wavy bitter-cress and patches of nettles. Other plants beside the stream include occasional water-mint, wood anemone, herb-Robert, creeping buttercup, lesser celandine, common valerian, tufted hair-grass and soft rush.

Over 2,500 trees have been planted, and their spacing will allow wildlife and wild flowers to thrive again in this historic wood pasture. The Forestry Commission has sold the removed conifers, and wood harvested on the estate now feeds a biomass boiler which provides heat and hot water for the castle and farm.

At the perimeter of the wood pasture is a pink gamekeeper's cottage (now a National Trust holiday cottage) – deer blood was traditionally mixed with whitewash to create the colour and protect its walls.

Opposite Fishpool Valley before restoration work began

Above The wood pasture after conifer extraction

The outer estate

Those walking the network of paths to the peripheral areas of the estate will find a rich flora and fauna to enjoy.

Bircher Common

Beyond Fishpool Valley is Bircher Common, a stretch of lowland dry acid grassland and scrub grazed by sheep, horses and a few cattle that incorporates old pollards, oak and birch trees. Further to the east lie Bircher Coppice and Oaker Coppice, an extensive area of unenclosed land at the north-eastern end of the estate with habitats including acid grassland, bracken, woodland and scrub, with ponds and veteran trees. Replanted ancient woodland areas contain a variety of native and non-native trees. Amongst the mature sessile oaks is a row of five ancient oak pollards. These two areas are managed to encourage habitats for invertebrates, fungi, birds and offer bat roosts. More recently reptile refuges have been placed around the area to encourage the expansion of the adder population.

Pokehouse Wood

To the west of the estate lies Pokehouse Wood, a narrow strip that occupies a west-facing slope above the River Lugg, with a small area of floodplain at the base. Herefordshire folklore suggests that Pokehouse could be a mutated form of Puckhse or 'Puck House' – Puck being an ill-meaning fairy. Local legend is that Puck would emerge after dark in these woods, and if he kidnapped someone they would never be seen again. A kind donor left a bequest so that the Aymestrey church bell could be rung before darkness fell each night, to warn people that they should escape the wood.

To the west of the estate lies Pokehouse Wood, a narrow strip that occupies a west-facing slope above the River Lugg, with a small area of floodplain at the base. The wood was given to the National Trust by Diana Uhlman. Much of Pokehouse Wood has been cleared of conifers to create open habitats which in its present form includes a large population of the plant wood vetch. Part of the replanting of native broadleaf trees in small fenced enclosures has been undertaken by children from a local school.

The River Lugg here is also designated a Site of Special Scientific Interest where you may be lucky enough to catch sight of otter, kingfisher and dipper. In late winter the banks of the river are a carpet of snowdrops. The track running adjacent to the river tends to remain damp and offers an environment that encourages sedges and rushes.

Left Remains of grain stores
on Croft Ambrey

The quarry in Pokehouse Wood is further indication of past industry. The nearby river could have been the means of transporting manufactured lime away from the two ruined lime kilns.

Croft Ambrey

The veteran trees support significant wood-decay invertebrate populations, notably the noble chafer beetle, along with important lichen communities. A series of veteran hawthorns also supports notable lichens, wood-decay invertebrates, and mistletoe with associated insects. The bracken needs controlling to allow flowers and grasses to survive and enhance the biodiversity. This is being done by two horses hauling a large roller which crushes the bracken, releasing cyanide and effectively poisoning itself, thereby stunting growth the following year. Eradicating the bracken is likely to take up to ten years.

Above Ancient trees on the walk up to Croft Ambrey from the castle

The Crofts of Croft Castle

Owners of Croft are shown in **bold**

* Denotes a portrait in the house

† Denotes a memorial in the church

Bernard de Croft
Held Croft in 1086

Sir Richard Croft † = Eleanor Mortimer †
(d. 1509) — née Cornwall (d. 1520)

Sir Edward Croft = Joyce
(d. 1547) — Skull

Richard Croft = Katherine
(d. 1562) — Herbert

Sir James Croft, MP* = (1) Alice Wigmore, née Warncombe (d. 1573) m. *c.*1540
(*c.*1518–90) — (2) Catherine Blount

Edward Croft, MP = Anne Browne
(d. 1601) — (d. 1575)

Sir Herbert Croft, MP = Mary
(1566–1629) — Bourne

Sir William Croft, MP
(1593–1645)

Sir James Croft
(d. 1659)

Dr Herbert Croft* = Anne
Bishop of Hereford (1603–91) — Browne

Elizabeth Croft*
(d. 1622)

Lucy Croft (*c.*1608–48) = Sir Dudley
grandmother of architect — Carleton
Sir John Vanbrugh

Sir Herbert Croft, MP* = Elizabeth Archer (d. 1709) m. 1675
cr.1st Bt 1671 (*c.*1652–1720) — sister of architect Thomas Archer

Sir Archer Croft, 2nd Bt, MP* = Frances Waring*
(1683–1753) *Sells Croft 1746* — (d. 1767) m. 1723

4 daughters

Francis Croft = Grace
(d. 1758) — Bramston

4 sons

Sir Archer Croft, 3rd Bt* = Elizabeth Cowper*
(1727–92) — (*c.*1737–1805) m. 1759

Sir John Croft, 4th Bt
(*c.*1735–97)

Herbert Croft = (1) Elizabeth Young
(1718–95) — (2) Mary Chawner

Rev. Sir Herbert Croft, 5th Bt* = (1) Sophia Cleave (d. 1792)
(1751–1816) *'Dictionary-maker'* — (2) Elizabeth Lewis (d. 1815) m. 1795

Sir Richard Croft, 6th Bt* = Margaret Denman
(1762–1818) *Royal physician* — (d. 1847)

Elizabeth Croft
(1769–1849)

Sir Thomas Croft, 7th Bt* = Sophia Lateward
(1798–1835) — (d. 1890) m. 1824

Sir Archer Croft, 8th Bt* = Julia Corbet
(1801–65) m. 1837 — (d. 1864)

Rev. Richard Croft = (1) Charlotte
(d. 1869) — Russell

Grace = Edward
(d. 1898) — Murray

Sir Herbert Croft, 9th Bt, MP* = Georgiana Marsh
(1838–1902) — m. 1865

Richard Croft = Anne
(d. 1912) of Fanhams Hall — Page

Bernard = Amy
Croft- — James
Murray

Sir Herbert = (1) Kathleen Hare
Croft, — (d. 1898) m. 1892
10th Bt — (2) Katherine
(1868–1915) — Parr m. 1903

Sir Hugh = Lucy
Croft, — Taylor
12th Bt*
(d. 1954)

Major = Stella
Owen — Bouwer
Croft,
(1880–1956)

Brig.-Gen. = Hon. Nancy
Sir Henry Page — Borwick
Croft, MP* — (1883–
1st LORD CROFT — 1949)
(1881–1947)

Lt. Col. = Eva
Richard — Stanhope
Page Croft
(d. 1956)

Edward
Croft-Murray

Sir James Croft, 11th Bt*
(1907–41) *His trustees buy
back Croft 1923*

Sir = Helen
Bernard — Weaver
Croft,
13th Bt

Michael, = Lady Antoinette
2nd Lord — Conyngham
Croft* — (d. 1959)
(1916–97) — m. 1948

Hon. = Fred
Diana — Uhlman
Croft

Major = Peggy
Richard — McClymont
Page
Croft

Bernard, 3rd Lord Croft* = Mary Richardson
(b. 1949) — m. 1993

Caroline

Hugo